LION LEADERSHIP MENTALITY

The Plan for Making Lion Leaders

LYNWOOD BATTS

ISBN 979-8-88685-499-2 (paperback)
ISBN 979-8-88685-500-5 (digital)

Christian Faith Publishing
832 Park Avenue
Meadville, PA 16335
www.christianfaithpublishing.com

Printed in the United States of America

CONTENTS

FOREWORD

You have heard the phrase, "Your arms are too short to box with the Lord." Well, that was the mantra that I served by and the Lord was true to His word. I was called to pastor a country church more than thirty years ago. It was in this church that the Lord Jesus, by the voice of the Holy Spirit, told me not to fight with the leaders of the church. I was told to teach them the Word, and by doing so, they would be able to choose right from wrong. They would learn that their fight was with the Lord and not with me, who was the servant of the Lord. Ultimately, the congregation began to grow in the knowledge of the Lord and to grow in the spirit of the Lord, and hence, they began to do things better together. This led to a growth in numbers and a growth financially, which allowed the building of a new church facility, youth ministry, women's ministry, men's ministry, missions ministry, clothing closet and food pantry, and much more.

LION LEADERSHIP

Abstract

It is paramount that a Lion leader understands passion, purpose, and vision, which leads to a plan. These steps will be paramount if the leader is intending to make disciples. Disciples are students of their teacher, and making disciples is the process of duplicating oneself in others by teaching them what your Lord has taught you. It is through this plan and vision that you carry on the teachings of Jesus Christ. If you, as a leader, do not receive the vision from the Lord, you will be stumbling around like a newborn deer, trying to stand for the first time. When you plan according to your passion, purpose, and vision, the Lord God will send others to join in the work with you. Those people resources the Lord God sends will join the effort with the passion required to fulfill the vision.

PREFACE

The first thirty-one years

For thirty years, I have been the senior pastor of Vaughn's Chapel, leading ministers, deacons, trustees, and the church family into a greater relationship with the Lord Jesus and each other. I also have more than thirty-five years of employment with *Fortune* 500 companies such as General Electric, Digital Equipment, and Cisco Systems, where I have participated in many leadership development courses and currently lead a sales team.

A lifelong passion

Leadership has been a passion since I was a teenager. My mother observed me and my cousins doing my chores of stacking wood on the front porch in the evenings after school. She said, "You could always get your friends to assist with your chores." She was telling me I was a leader even as a teenager. I would make the work of chopping wood a competition, meaning who could chop a block of wood with one swing of the axe and who could carry the most wood In their arms in one trip. It did not seem much like work to us teenagers; it was fun.

Fun is a keyword for leadership. How do you make serving and leading others fun? What procedures do you have in place to take the feeling of work out of the process of ministry? Those questions and answers are typically right in front of your eyes when you, as a leader, are taught how to adjust your lens to see them.

Leadership development over the years

I have participated in many leadership development courses over the years and have a Master of Science Degree in Leadership from Northeastern University and a Master of Arts in Biblical Studies, which allows me to bridge the gap between ministry and leadership.

The *Lion Leadership Mentality* is a book that focuses on leading like a lion while understanding what makes a lion survive in the world that he was born to reign in. The lion mentality is about more than being the strongest, the fastest, or the biggest but developing the attitude of the lion. When you are driven by passion, purpose, and vision, you will begin to understand why all the other animals fear the lion. God has planted in the DNA of the lion the will to survive and to teach this concept to those that will follow. The lion is the king because he knows what it takes to make it through another day. He teaches this strategy to those who will follow and desire to develop the lion mentality.

The concept of lion leadership was born out of my desire to watch documentaries that explored the life of a lion. This knowledge of the lion merged with my passion for leadership and my passion for biblical studies. When both biblical studies come together with leadership studies and the attitude of the lion, you get the "lion mentality."

INTRODUCTION

A *lion* is the king of the jungle, every animal knows it. The lion is not the fastest or biggest. The cheetah is the fastest, and the elephant is the biggest. However, the lion looks at the elephant and sees lunch, which puts fear in the elephant's heart. The cheetah keeps its distance from the lion because the lion will kill it to preserve food in its territory. My fascination with the lion and my love for the Lord God, my Father in heaven, and His Son and my Savior, Jesus, and the indwelling power of the Holy Spirit has led me to write and develop this concept, the Lion Leadership mentality. If we as leaders would nurture the lion mentality or the lion attitude toward survival, we would make greater strides as leaders.

A Lion leader is a person that has a purpose, a vision, and a plan that is driven by a passion that has been imposed upon them by someone of greater authority, God almighty. "God so love the world that He gave His only begotten Son" (John 3:16). It is God's love that demonstrates His *passion* for the human race and world, which led to the virgin birth of Jesus into this world with the *purpose* of giving His life for all mankind. With the purpose came the *plan* and the command to resurrect His life, therefore redeeming man back to God. It is in Genesis 3:14–15 that we see the *vision* of God bringing forth a seed that will bruise the head of Satan. This *vision* was fulfilled in Jesus the Christ as the redeemer of the human race.

Furthermore, every man, woman, and child should have both a purpose, a vision, and a plan for their lives that is driven by passion. However, the average leader does not explore their purpose, vision, and plan because most leaders have not been taught how to recognize or develop the Lion leader. The leader must learn what questions to ask, even within themselves, to develop the Lion leader within themselves. Questions like, who am I? Why am I here? What is my purpose? What am I passionate about? Answers to questions like these will assist a Lion mentality in coming forth. This allows the Lion leader to take his or her rightful position in leadership. Let's pause and answer these questions:

1. Who am I? (This is your brand.) _________________

\
\
\

2. Why am I here on earth, or what am I here to do?

\
\
\

3. What is my purpose? (May be the same as number 2.)

\
\
\

4. What am I passionate about? (This is what drives you.)

\
\
\

Jesus took Peter, James, John, and nine others and made them disciples. He called them from their professions for three and a half years to teach them how to enhance their skills to become fishers of men. Notice, He did not make them abandon their professional knowledge and skills entirely but utilized what they knew to be true and enveloped it with His passion, purpose, and plan, therefore making it *their* passion, purpose, and plan. That is what Lion leaders do;

they help you to find your passion and purpose, see your vision, and fulfill the plan God has established for your life. In doing so, it connects you with and fulfills your purpose, vision, and plan.

The Lion leader is also a person that you are drawn to. Lion leaders have the ability to gain the interest of others while developing them to lead in their absence. A Lion leader will leave a legacy, and the hope of the Lion leader is to have someone carry on that legacy long after they are gone. Also, a Lion leader is a thinker and looks to have people in the immediate leadership circle that can think for themselves, assisting to fulfill the passion, purpose, vision, and plan as he continues to seek opportunities to glorify God, the author and finisher of our faith. This was a key aspect of Jesus; His purpose was to glorify the Father that sent Him. A Lion leader is focused not on himself but the betterment of those around him and gives credit to those who support him. Therefore, a Lion leader is not selfish and does not work for selfish gain but considers others more esteemed than himself. This principle is met with great reward and blessing from the Lord and from those that are developed under his/her leadership. In the simplest form, the Lion leader develops other Lion leaders to carry on the vision and plan that has been initiated.

What we are doing in this book is looking to assist you in nurturing the Lion leadership mentality and identifying the potential Lion leaders among you and teaching those Lion leaders to make other Lion leaders. When we can adopt the mentality of a lion and then duplicate this mentality, we are basically doing what Jesus called "making disciples and teaching them to observe all that I have taught you" (Matthew 28:18–21). Developing Lions, or Lion leaders, is a serious task, and this is a responsibility that falls squarely upon the shoulders of the church leadership or the leadership of the organization that a Lion leader works for. However, if church leadership is not schooled in how to make Lion leaders, they could be in for a long and hard ministry where the pastor and a few others carry the load of the church.

I speak from experience; I have seen too many strong, anointed men and women of God burn out because there is much to do and too few Lion leaders to get it done. Jesus said, "The harvest is plentiful but the labors are few. Pray to the Lord of the harvest to send more laborers into His harvest" (Luke 10:1–2). Asking the Lord or owner of the harvest to send more laborers is vitally important to the Lions. But it is important that the Lion leader is able to recognize who the Lord of the harvest has sent to assist with the harvest because the person sent may not be what you expect or who you expect. There was a time when we needed assistance in the music ministry, and the Lord sent someone from a neighboring state to come in and teach voice to the choir. It was an awesome experience and valued by the choir members because this Lion leader of music pushed them to reach new heights that would not have been reached had the Lion leader not been from outside of the congregation. Corporations do this all the time, bringing in someone that has special skills to assist in developing the leaders as they attempt to meet the purpose, vision, and plan of the organization.

An example of Lion leadership is recorded in 1 Samuel 17, when David faces Goliath. The army of Israel was afraid to fight the Philistines because of this nearly ten-foot giant of a man, Goliath. If you can't face the giant in your life, how can you defeat the army behind the giant? David had experience with the lion and the bear, killing both because he was under the covenant of God, and under this covenant, He knew he was protected by the God of the covenant. David saw Goliath as an opportunity to glorify the Lord God, and this he did.

David's Lion leadership after the defeat of Goliath caused the Israelite army to gain courage and attack the Philistines and defeat them. That is a characteristic of Lion leaders; they inspire and encourage those around them to take on the giants and defeat the armies that defy the Lord God almighty. When you have a Lion leader in front of a fearful army, this courageous Lion leader, by the victory over the giant of the opposing army who dared threaten the execution of his purpose, vision, and plan, will cause the fear to disappear and the Lion mentality to arise in the hearts of those followers to become courageous men and women.

SECTION 1

The Lion Mentality

"An army of sheep led by lions will always defeat an army of lions led by sheep," words originally stated by Alexander the Great. When you visualize this statement, you can almost see a lion leading a flock of sheep, figuratively speaking, for lions *do* eat sheep. A sheep is a person that will follow a purpose, vision, and plan but needs to be led by a Lion leader that is walking in his/her purpose, vision, and plan. Sheep are defined as those who desire to be led but by a Lion leader that has a purpose, vision, and plan.

When David said in the Psalm 23, "The Lord is my Shepherd," he was speaking as a man who was to be King over Israel from an early age. David was not cowardly. He was brave because of how the Lord God had taught and delivered him through experiences with both the lion and the bear that came to devour his sheep. You see, within this sheep, there is a Lion leader waiting to emerge and make and lead other lions. The sheep just needs the opportunity and the occasion to lead while being nurtured by a Lion leader.

The Lion leader will lead the sheep to victory because the lion's mentality of victory and survival has been transferred to the sheep. With the Lion leader's mentality toward survival, the sheep change their natural skittish demeanor and become brave and ferocious leaders with purpose, vision and a plan. The **Lion Mentality** for success is passed on to the flock of sheep that he/she is leading and the team adopts this mentality which changes their behavior. If I could explain the concept from a Hollywood point of view, you would see a Lion leading a flock of sheep that were transforming as they went into Lions, adopting the Lion mentality as their own. The Lion leader would glance back to not see sheep forging ahead but Lion leaders with the same passion, purpose, vision and plan.

David was such a lion of a leader that he had followers who performed some amazing feats. For example, Benaiah, son of Jehoiada, according to 2 Samuel 23:20–21, was such a warrior. To his credit, "he went into a pit on a snowy day and killed a lion, and then killed an Egyptian by slaying him with his own sword." That was not all. He became the leader of David's bodyguards and walked among the thirty mighty warriors in David's army, though he was not named among the three mightiest warriors, Josheb-Basshebeth (the chief of the three), Eleazar, and Shammah. These men had done some great things as empowered by the Lord God. David was the Lion leader who drew to him great men, who took on his passion and purpose. They would not only defend him to the end but also adopt David's purpose, vision, and plan, making it their own. That is what great Lion leaders do; their passion and purpose invite others to join their cause, fighting alongside them on the battlefield of life and giving their life if necessary.

The Lion Mentality comes from one's passion. Passion is that internal desire to do and complete something, even when you can see the difficulties associated with it. The lion looks out over the plains at thousands of animals, including hundreds of gazelles, which could be overwhelming for the average hunter. However, the lion narrows hundreds of gazelles down to one, and he focuses on that one. The strategy then takes shape as the lions strategically put all their energy into executing the plan of separating one gazelle from the hundreds. As they work out the strategy, each lioness has a role to play, and they do it perfectly. One lioness flanks the gazelle, the other pushes from behind, and another lion waits in the tall grass for the gazelle to be driven in her direction. When the time is right, that lioness leaps out of the tall grass, digging its long claws into the flesh, and finally locking its jaws around the gazelle's, throat cutting off its air. Once on the ground, the gazelle is helpless as the other lions come to join in on the kill. Wow! What a completely successful strategy.

What drives them all? Their passion does. Passion drives their mentality toward life and goals to sustain life. It is because a lion has a passion for its own survival and the survival of its pride, including its offspring. Because of this passion and purpose, it is determined to do what is necessary to stay alive for another day. As a leader, you adopt the Lion leader mentality and pass it along to your pride or team; they will adopt your passion and follow you as you lead them with the lion mentality. Additionally, other Lion leaders will look to join your pride, bringing with them all of their passions. A Lion Leader must expect and be ready to embrace Lions from different prides, teams, organizations, or churches.

Section 2

The Making of a Lion Leader

Great leaders get great results from those that follow them. According to John Zenger and Joseph R. Folkman's research in *The Extraordinary Leader*, an extraordinary leader is able to attract, retain, and influence those that follow them to produce much higher results as a leader. Great leaders focus on the strengths of those they lead, and this process helps to build a strong team. Next, the leader focuses on the personal needs of the follower and attempts to fulfill those needs. Finally, the leader focuses on the development of the follower, which feeds into their personal development. Thereby, giving the follower a sense of belonging while seeing the value they bring to the team as a whole.

Throughout this book, we will explore four main attributes of outstanding leadership. Lion leaders have *passion* which guides their purpose, vision, and plan.

1. Lion leaders have *passion*, which is something that you wake up thinking about and can't seem to put it to the side without it coming back into your mind again.

2. Lion leaders have a *purpose*, which is the catalyst to everything that they do.
3. Lion leaders have a *vision* for survival and success—without a vision, people perish.
4. Lion leaders build a *plan*. Lion leaders understand that building trusting relationships is key to the success of the purpose and vision. Lion leaders also know that trust is the by-product of their actions and behaviors.

The lion has, within its DNA, a complete library as to who and what it is and what it is to accomplish every day of its life. The lion wakes up with the purpose of surviving another day by providing food for itself and the pride. Though there is plenty of food on the plains of Africa, the prey does not stand still to be caught. Much work must be done by the lion to catch its daily food. The gazelle is not a predator or hunter, so it wakes up expecting to be hunted and strives to not get eaten.

You have seen above the mention of passion, purpose, vision, and planning, which I will dive deeper into in the following pages. It is paramount as a Lion leader that you understand and answer each of the following questions if you are going to walk with a Lion mentality.

Step 1: Passion

What is *passion*? Passion is that strong intrinsic attachment that you have to something that intrigues you, causing you to spend significant time thinking and talking about it. It is important that you spend time fine-tuning your passion by reading books that pertain to your passion and surrounding yourself with those of like passion.

Jesus makes it clear that His passion came from the Father, and the Father's passion, or love, was that man would have a savior that would redeem man back to Him. Jesus chooses twelve disciples to follow Him, and He has to get these chosen disciples to take on this passion and make it their own. When we, as Lion leaders, learn how to transfer our passion to the men and women that we lead, we will then have men and women that will lead, even when we are not in their presence.

What is your passion? As a Lion leader, your passion will reveal your purpose. As you discover your passion, it will help in the discovery of your purpose. Passion is defined as a strong feeling that you have for something. Answer this question: What do you just enjoy doing? It is probably something that you get the utmost joy out of performing or just talking about with others. Something that you think is trivial because it comes easily to you, others see value in it and would love to have you and your passion/gift on their team and in their organization. Discover your passion and you will be well on your way to understanding your purpose.

Many times, we want to direct men by appealing to their physical need to be stimulated by a hammer and nail. Jesus led by presenting a purpose for following Him, and with the purpose, He also had a plan. Jesus needed followers that would be willing to learn and carry on the purpose, vision, and plan when He was resurrected. The longer these disciples remained with Him, the more His purpose would be revealed. The purpose was developed out of His passion for the love of the Father and the love of the world. Jesus had three and a half years to share and impose this passion on the disciples, thereby making His purpose their passion. This is one thing that Lion leaders must learn to do, share their passion. What is your passion as a Lion leader? If you identify your passion and begin to share your passion with others, people will begin to buy into your purpose and plan.

King David's passion for leadership grew in the midst of shepherding the sheep for which he was responsible. 1 Samuel 17:34–36 gives us the account of David explaining to King Saul that he was more than just a youth in comparison to Goliath, the giant Philistine. David confesses that he has killed a bear and a lion that came to feast on the sheep that he was given responsibility to shepherd. David's passion to provide safety, support, and nurturing to the sheep will be beneficial to him as a future king of Israel. David understood that his success with both the bear and the lion was fueled by the grace and covenant of God Almighty.

This passion is what gave David purpose, and passion is why he could walk past the Israelite army to face the giant Goliath with only a slingshot and rocks. Passion allows you to see what is possible, especially when you have experiences from the Lord God Jehovah at your side. When you accept your passion, it will reveal your purpose. Once you understand your passion, you will understand what you are here on earth to accomplish. Passion makes you more assertive than others in the same room, army, or situation. Passion causes you to face your giants with only what's in your hands. However, keep in mind that there will be obstacles, and the enemy does not lie down just because you discovered what you are passionate about. You will more than ever need to fight like a lion protecting its pride or family if you wish to see the vision and plan executed. Take a moment to answer the questions below to assist you with identifying your passion.

What do you enjoy doing? Why?

____

____

____

____

____

I am passionate about:

____

____

____

____

____

Step 2: Purpose

What is *purpose*? Purpose is the reason why you, as a Lion leader, get up in the morning and seek to do something that will change the world around you for the betterment of others. Who does it benefit, and what benefit will you and your followers receive? John 3:16 sums up the purpose very well: "God so loved the world that He gave His only begotten Son, that whosoever believe on Him, they shall never perish but have everlasting life." The purpose was pretty clear to anyone that would listen. God the Father wanted to deliver man from the curse of sin and the law. The only way to do that was to have someone that was holy to die and resurrect. Therefore, in John 10:18, God the Father commanded that Jesus "lay down His life but pick it up again." Within the purpose was the plan to resurrect, and without the resurrecting power, the plan would have been incomplete.

As a Lion leader, understanding your purpose helps to develop a vision and plan that will sustain life for you and your family in the coming years. According to *National Geographic*, the life expectancy of a lion in the wild is about fifteen years; therefore, his vision and plan must exceed fifteen years. The human life expectancy is eighty to ninety years; therefore, our vision and plan must exceed that life span. However, many of us rarely consider life beyond our twenties because no one has suggested such a thing. That is where purpose comes in; when I understand my purpose, I am able to develop a vision and plan.

As a Lion leader, you must begin with a solid foundation of who you are and where you are going. Without this foundation, a Lion leader can and will get sidetracked or derailed. Let's explore each of these:

Who are you? To determine who you are, you must consider your creator, why the creator created you, and for what purpose. You can find many of these answers in the scriptures and from honest self-evaluation. It also helps to have someone that can guide you through this discovery by asking the powerful probing questions that we don't want to answer. Many times, who we are is hidden in what we are running from or scared of becoming. I discovered that I love to teach, edify, and see the eyes of students illuminate with the advent of new knowledge or nuggets of information. I did not receive a degree in education but discovered my passion when I began to pastor thirty years ago. Teaching Bible study and Sunday school to the youth of the church became so rewarding. It is because of this passion that I wrote this book and why I went back to school to get an MA in biblical studies and an MS in leadership.

I am now combining both degrees to give Lion leaders the opportunity to emerge from the depths of the sheep skin while developing the Lions Mentality. In Genesis 2:11–15, Moses discovers who he is. He is not an Egyptian but a Hebrew. His people are in bondage while he is growing up in the luxury of Pharaoh's house. Moses kills an Egyptian that is mistreating a Hebrew, and now he must flee because Pharaoh seeks to kill him. It is in this fleeing that we find that Moses has passion for his people and God Almighty will use this passion to further help Moses see that he is the Lion leader that has been chosen to lead His people out of bondage.

Where are you going? In Exodus 3:1–11, Moses discovered his purpose on the backside of the mountain of God, when he met the God of his fathers in the burning bush. God called Moses to be a messenger that would be the instrument in His hands, to lead and deliver the children of Israel out of bondage in Egypt. Once Moses knew that he was a messenger for the Lord, he needed a message. The Lord God gave him the message to give to Pharaoh: "Let my people go." God gave him a rod, not just any rod, but one that would be used to demonstrate the power of God to the Egyptians. As you can see, once you have your purpose and know who you are or who you are called to be, resources are made available to you and results are guaranteed by God who anointed you for the mission or task.

People will come to your aid when you *reveal your purpose*. I have noticed that people will donate, volunteer, or even pay for your services when they see and understand that you are operating with a purpose. The reason is because you are able to articulate the vision and the plan associated with it. You don't come across as a fly-by-night leader that is making it up as you go. You see, purpose is a strong driving force that motivates others who are seeking something to undergird and support. Take some time to reveal your purpose and watch others seek you out to understand what you are meant to do.

The following are questions you can answer to identify your purpose:

a. Based upon my passion, what am I purposed to do?
b. Based upon my trials and tribulations, what purpose has been identified?
c. What benefit will others receive from my purpose?
d. Why did God put me here on in this ministry, organization, or town?
e. Where are your going?

Step 3: Vision

The next foundational step is to have a vision. A vision is a picture in your mind and heart of what you want the future to be. Out of that vision comes a plan that can be implemented to fulfill its purpose. We see vision appear in scripture as well. In Numbers 12:6, "the Lord made Himself known to the prophet in a vision and God will speak to the prophet in a dream." The Word of the Lord said, "Where there is no vision which means where there is no revelation of God or of His word, the people perish or are restrained" (Proverbs 29:18). The vision for the future was paramount to the servants and prophets of God. If a vision from God is so important, why do church leaders operate so often without a vision? Why do individuals and families operate without a vision for themselves and their families? Because we have been conditioned in this instant society to live one day at a time!

The Bible says a lot about worry or not to worry, when you can bring all things to the Lord in prayer (Philippians 4:6). When you pray, you should not worry or be anxious about nothing because you know as a leader that God our Lord will provide. If the vision came from the Lord, it is the Lord's plan and vision. Because it is the Lord's vision, the Lord God maintains the responsibility to carry out the vision through you to its completion. The reason the Lord is using you is because you are a present and willing vessel here on earth and you are filled with the Holy Spirit of God. You are authorized and empowered to operate here on earth, just as Jesus operated here on earth before His death, burial, and resurrection.

As a Lion leader, the first thing you must do is seek a vision from the Lord. Once that vision has been given by the Lord God, then you can write it down. If you have heard from the Lord and have a vision, take a moment to write it down and make it plain on the following page. I have included additional steps to assist you more in fully developing your Lion Mentality. Use the space below to outline your vision.

My vision is ____

As a leader, I am / will be _______________________________

As a leader, I want to __________________________________

____

____

As a leader, I want to achieve _____________________________

____

A vision is made up of several specific factors, like: mission statement, objectives, strategies, tactics, and resources. We will briefly explore each of them in the following pages in the section with the plan. Make sure you write a response to each step below.

Mission Statement is a statement identifying the purpose and the vision you have been given by a higher authority, Jehovah God. In Matthew 28:18–20, Jesus comes to the disciples, declaring that "He has all power in His hands in heaven and earth, go ye therefore, and teach all nations, baptizing them in the name of the Father, and of the Son, and of the Holy Ghost:"

My mission is ____

____

____

Step 4: Plan

What's a *plan*? A plan is a series of steps required to complete a purpose and vision. When leading people, you need a plan that accomplishes the purpose. When the plan is complete, it gives the men a road map as to what to expect next. When people have a plan, even if it is verbal, they are able to see where they are going and how to get there. This was important to fishermen because, while on the ship in the sea, they needed to navigate their course so they would not lose their bearings, allowing them to return back home safely.

Objectives are a collection of goals that are required to make your purpose and vision come to life. The objective in the mission statement is to go teach and baptize all nations. Teaching all nations must be broken down into smaller digestible chunks, like going to Corinth and Ephesus. These become your objectives. Therefore, objective one was teaching and baptizing those that were converted in Corinth and Ephesus in the name of the Father and the Son and the Holy Ghost. Again, the lion can't chase the entire herd of gazelles; therefore, he reduces the size of the herd to one gazelle he can pursue, capture, and devour.

My objectives are _________________________________
____
____

Strategies are the all-encompassing plans of action that you will execute to make the purpose and vision come to fruition. The strategy is closely aligned to the purpose and the vision. Remember, the lion's objective is to separate the one gazelle from the hundreds. His strategy is to make the gazelle run into his trap without revealing his purpose of eating dinner.

My strategy is __________________________________
____
____

Tactics are the short-term steps that you take to execute a strategy. The lion will strategically move the gazelle away from the herd. If you ask how this is accomplished, you are on the right track to tactical awareness. The lion has three tactics: engage, separate, and attack. One lion engages the gazelle, causing it to run. The other will flank the gazelle, causing it to turn in the desired direction, away from the herd. Yet a third lion will wait in the tall grass, waiting for the gazelle to come running by; then it will attack. All these tactics are required to make the hunting strategy successful.

My tactics are ____

____

____

Resources required: Resources are all the tools required to make the vision and plan come to life. This includes people resources. Resources are vitally important to the success of the purpose, vision, and plan. What resources are required to make all these come together? The lion has several resources at his disposal: supporting lions, gazelle's fear, tall grass for camouflage, and his own critical thinking and problem-solving skills. The Lion leaders use people resources, marketing resources, specialty skills resources, and the internet to get things in the position required to be successful.

My required resources are _______________________________________

____

____

Time required to complete the plan: Time affects everything. How much time will it take to get the gazelle in the right position is part of the mentality of the lion. Lions are not meant to chase the gazelle for long periods of time because distance running is to the advantage of the gazelle. If you don't establish a time table for completion, you may never see the fulfillment of your purpose and vision. Too many times, we hesitate to implement a time line for completion of our projects. As a result, the project gets delayed, postponed, and sometimes abandoned all together. If you adopt the Lion Mentality, you will welcome a time line because it lets you and the team know that you are seriously committed to the purpose, vision, and plan. Jesus did more in three and a half years than we do in a lifetime. Imagine what we would accomplish if we took full advantage of the time given in a lifetime.

Time allotted is a necessity but is most underutilized in our approach to fulfilling the vision that is laid before us. Time is given in days, months, and years and counted in milliseconds, seconds, minutes, and hours. However, there are only twenty-four hours in a day, and we sleep approximately seven to eight of those hours each day. When we gain an understanding of time and the value of time, we will become motivated by the lack of time and be intentional with the time that we are given. We take time for granted, and God our Father presents time as an opportunity and a season. Ecclesiastes states that there is a time and a season for everything. You only have so much time before it is time for something else. As a leader, what are you doing with the time that has been allotted to you? Take some time to complete your timetable.

I will set a timetable for the completion of: _______________

____

____

____

Conclusion: As you adopt the Lion Mentality, you will find the above steps valuable to your success as a leader. It is important to keep these steps in mind as you share your purpose, vision, and plan because it will show the church leadership or organization that you have given much thought to the project at hand. You will also find that others will join your purpose when you can properly articulate it. There are many Lions around you waiting to join the vision that the Lord has given you, and there are other Lions that will come out of the sheep's skin, so to speak, when you give them a reason to roar.

Section 3

Five Elements of Lion Leadership

This section will deal with the elements of leadership that the Lion leader must have to lead and build a lasting relationship with those that follow. I have selected the following five elements of leadership: value, action, skills, knowledge, and planning.

Element 1: Value

The first of these elements is value. This element of leadership is discovering, exploring, or revealing your values and understanding what role your values play in your leadership skills. Values are those things on which you will not compromise because they make you who you are. Values are those things that you will stand on, no matter what arises, and every good leader must plant their feet firmly on these uncompromising values. Jesus helps us with understanding values when He said, "Father if you are willing, remove this cup from me. Yet not My will but your will be done" (Luke 22:42–45). Jesus valued the relationship with the Father so much that he surrendered his will even unto death. But even more importantly, Jesus's value system was based upon the value system of His Father in heaven. Therefore, you should develop your value system around those values of our Father who is in heaven.

This example of Jesus's will to please the Father was passed down to the disciples. If they were going to successfully carry out the mission of making more disciples and carrying the gospel to the world, they needed to understand their values and compare them to the values of the Lion of Judah, Jesus the Christ. If they did not have the values of Jesus, they would risk damaging the reputation of Jesus and preventing the furtherance of the gospel, as it was to be shared with the Jews and the Gentiles. The disciples had values like trust, commitment, faithfulness, and loyalty, to name a few. These values would be the catalysts to their success in the furtherance of the gospel and the great commission.

David is referred to by God as "a man after His own heart" (Acts 13:22). This simply means that David's purposes, plans, and will were those of the Lord God Almighty. David, even in sin, would run to God in prayer, asking for forgiveness. David knew something about his values that when he compromised his relationship with Jehovah God, through prayer and repentance, Jehovah God was the only one that could deliver him from himself. The Lion mentality is one that seeks to do right even when the temptation is there to do wrong. Paul demonstrated this in Romans 7:21–25 when he explained the desire to do good, but evil was ever present and there was a war going on between his inner man and his outer man. What wretched man I am, he exclaimed! But thanks be to God through Jesus Christ who has delivered him and us all.

List of values from intentional life coaching

On the following page, you will find a list of values that may assist you in recognizing those values that represent you as an individual. Select those values that represent you and that will assist you in becoming a Lion leader.

Accomplishment, Success	Democracy	Gratitude	Patriotism	Self-reliance
Accountability	Discipline	Hard work	Peace	Sensitivity
Accuracy	Discovery	Happiness	Perfection	Service
Adventure	Diversity	Harmony	Personal Growth	Simplicity
Beauty	Dynamism	Health	Perseverance	Solving Problems
Calm, quietude,	Ease of Use	Honor	Pleasure	Speed
Challenge	Efficiency	Human-centered	Power	Spirit/ Spirituality
Change	Enjoyment	Improvement	Practicality	Stability
Charity	Equality	Independence	Preservation	Standardization
Cleanliness, orderliness	Excellence	Individuality	Privacy	Status
Collaboration	Fairness	Inner peace	Progress	Strength
Commitment	Faith	Innovation	Prosperity, Wealth	Succeed/ Success
Communication	Faithfulness	Integrity	Punctuality	Systemization
Community	Family	Intelligence	Quality of work	Teamwork
Competence	Family feeling	Justice	Reliability	Timeliness
Competition	Freedom, Liberty	Kindness	Resourcefulness	Tolerance
Concern for others	Friendship	Knowledge	Respect for others	Tradition
Connection	Fun	Leadership	Responsiveness	Tranquility
Cooperation	Generosity	Love, Romance	Results-oriented	Trust
Coordination	Gentleness	Loyalty	Rule of Law	Truth
Creativity	Global view	Meaning	Safety	Unity
Decisiveness	Goodwill	Merit	Satisfying others	Well-being
Determination	Goodness	Money	Security	Wisdom

One of the values that I brought with me into ministry was peace. I was not called to the pastorate to fight with God's people. I stood by the value of peace and promoted peace for thirty years of pastorate because the Holy Spirit led me to conclude that the Word of God was a much better weapon against traditional strongholds than me standing toe-to-toe with a church leader, and arguing was not an option. I also concluded that if I continued to teach the Word of God, they would conclude, as I did, that their arms were too short to box with God. Therefore, even though I was sent by God to be the pastor, the congregation belonged to God the Father. What a relief it was when it was revealed to me that the congregation of believers were not owned by me but were the people of Jehovah, our Father and God.

My values are: ____
____
____
____

Element 2: Action

Your passion, purpose, vision, and values must be followed by your actions. Your actions are a visible manifestation of your vision and values. The way you relate to and treat those that follow you will reveal your character. Your character will help followers determine your ethics and if you are trustworthy.

In James 1:21–25, we are told to lay aside all filthiness and overflow of wickedness and receive with meekness the implanted word of God that is able to save our souls. It is this Word of God that we, as Lion leaders, must embrace because it is this Word of God that will give us life. By doing more than talking, a Lion leader demonstrates to the followers that the leader believes what they are saying.

There is an old saying, "Let the life I live speak for me." This phrase has been handed down from generation to generation with the meaning that one must be a living example of their values, and more importantly, Christian values. If you, as a lion leader, desire someone to follow you, then you must be an example so they can have confidence in you as a Lion leader. If you want the floor swept, then, as a Lion leader, you must pick up the broom and begin to sweep. I found by doing this, someone would ask if they could sweep and or even take the broom from me and finish the job of sweeping the floor.

As a Lion leader, don't ask someone to do what you are not willing to do. Jesus gave His life so we would have life, and, therefore, asks us to be a living sacrifice unto God. He did not and has not asked us to die for anyone. As a matter of biblical fact, it says, "Greater love has no man than this, that he will lay down his life for his friends" (John 15:13). Jesus set an example of love for us and, therefore, we are an example, and our actions will lead others to be like us or better yet, be like Jesus, the Lion of Judah.

If you observe a pride of lions, you will find this common thread: their actions are developed out of their purpose to survive. They demonstrate these actions every day of their lives, and these actions are passed down to the next generation along with the purpose that must be carried on. The lion's strategic approach to catching the gazelle is the same day after day. What actions in your leadership arsenal are repeatable? What actions do you want to refine? What actions have you seen in others that will assist you with achieving your goals? These are a few questions that are worth answering.

Questions

1. What actions are you willing to take as a leader to demonstrate your values and character?

2. What key characteristics do you possess that represent who you are and how you treat others?

3. What actions do you want to refine, and what actions are worth repeating?

4. What actions in your leadership arsenal are repeatable?

5. What actions do you want to refine?

6. What actions have you seen in others that will assist you
    with achieving your goals?

———————————————, ————————————————,

———————————————, ————————————————,

———————————————, ————————————————

Element 3: Skills and knowledge

Skills and knowledge are important to a leader if they plan to
grow the ministry or the organization. Why skills and why knowledge? A person with skills has a particular expertise that can be utilized to assist with a purpose, vision, and plan. When a person has
skills, it is up to the leader to understand those skills, prayerfully, for
the betterment of the ministry and the implementation of the vision.
Knowledge in and of itself is only the ability to learn, but when you
can apply what you know, you are operating in wisdom.

If Lion leaders are not careful, they will try to do everything
themselves and not allow others to participate because they have
determined that no one can do it the way it should be done. When
this occurs, you will feel like you are in it alone and you don't have
a team. The potential laborers feel like you don't want them on the
team, so they back away, find somewhere else to work, and many
times leave your ministry or organization all together.

It takes a skillful Lion leader to recognize talent and then put
that talent to work, especially, when you, as a Lion leader, feel threat-
ened. In Matthew 25:14, the story of the servants and the talents is
told. There was one servant who buried the talent in what seemed to
be a fear of losing it. Of course, this servant was punished for doing
nothing. The focus should be on the master (Lion), who trusted each
servant with a sum of money to invest. Apparently, each servant had
a skill, but the servant with one talent became afraid and hid the
money, thinking he understood the master. Is that how those around
you feel about you? Are they afraid to make a mistake? If so, you
must help them relax and exercise their gift.

It is okay to make mistakes; we all do, and that is how we grow and learn. If you were to talk to any inventor, they would tell you how many times they failed before developing a successful invention that brought fame and fortune. Failure is a part of the process of learning, but as Lion leaders, we get impatient with followers and are ready to remove them before giving them a chance to develop and strengthen their skills.

When hunting, a lion does not make a successful kill every time. The conditions have to be just right to catch a gazelle. For example, the element of surprise is key to their success. Therefore, tall grass is an advantage, which allows cover along with the direction of the wind. This knowledge and skill that the lion utilizes to his advantage, along with other natural elements, plays a part in the lion's success. The point is, as a Lion leader, you must develop the skills and knowledge, including surrounding yourself with people resources who understand the terrain that you are navigating.

The concept of strength-based leadership, as discussed in the book *Now Discover Your Strength* by Buckingham and Clifton PhD, is a relatively new concept within the last twenty years or so. This idea focuses on a person's strength, which can also be an area of passion. When a leader focuses on the strengths of an individual, they give the follower the opportunity to grow faster because they are allowed to focus on one thing that they enjoy doing and can do well.

When it comes to knowledge, I say, "I don't know everything, but I know someone that knows everything." What I mean is, if I don't know the answer, the Lord God knows the answer, and He directs me to someone that can answer my questions. As a Lion leader, you don't have to know everything, but prayerfully, build a circle of people that can assist with the passion, purpose, vision, and plan.

Question: What self-investments do you want to make to improve your leadership skills and knowledge?

____

____

____

Question: What materials, including books, do you need to become a better informed, skilled, and knowledgeable leader?

—————————————————, ————————————————————,

—————————————————, ————————————————————,

—————————————————, ————————————————————.

Element 4: Relationships

This brings us to a vital point in leading teams, relationships. Developing a relationship with the members of the team is vital to your success. A relationship is a connection between two or more people. When people connect for a common goal and objective, they walk in the biblical principle of "touching and agreeing," according to Matthew 18:19. The touching and agreeing of two or more ushers in the very presence of the Lord God Jesus Christ, as we pray on earth. Therefore, as a Lion leader you can see how relationships are so important to the vision and plan being executed here on earth. You can also see how important unity is here on earth. When we touch and agree, we are legally saying we are bearing witness to this prayer and even the vision. When two or more touch and agree, we are able to bind whatsoever here on earth, and when that happens, it binds whatsoever in heaven according to the will of God. This means that heaven agrees with what we have bound on earth; therefore, God the Father moves on our behalf here on earth.

The same is true about what we loose on earth. It causes that thing to be loosed by heaven's standards, which is echoed here on earth. This is a powerful principle that is many times misunderstood by the leadership and its followers. When we agree on the purpose, vision, and plan, we are requesting God Almighty to intervene in His purpose, vision, and plan, releasing the Holy Spirit and power to move with actionable resources in our lives. There are many examples of the children of Israel where Jehovah intervened and gave them victory over the enemy. As long as Moses held up his arms in Exodus 17:12–14, the Amelak warriors were defeated. Was the victory in the arms alone or in the resources that the Lord sent to fight with Joshua and the Israelite army, or did Jehovah send angels to fight with them? What we know is that the army of Israel won the battle, and Moses had to do his part, and the people of Israel had to go on the battlefield to receive the victory.

Element 5: Influence and inspire

As a Lion leader, you will also influence and inspire others. Influence means that you have an effect on the character and behavior of those that you lead. Influence can be very subtle and executed without a strong command. We influence others when we allow them to remain in our presence to learn from us. People are influenced because they trust you and believe you have their best interest in mind. Jesus said, "All you who are heavy laden, come to me and take my yoke upon you and learn of me" (Matthew 11:28–30). This invitation to learn about Him was welcomed with the benefit of gaining rest. Jesus was able to influence those around him by His actions and teachings. Twelve men who did not grow up with him, accepted the call to discipleship and trusted Him for three and a half years. After that, they took on his passion and purpose and continued the message of the kingdom of God.

Another good example of influence and inspiration is the relationship between Elijah and Elisha. Elisha was aware of God Almighty's servant Elijah and how the Lord God was using him, that he wanted a double portion of Elijah's anointing. He was so influenced and inspired by Elijah that he agreed to follow him on his daily quest. Therefore, Elijah invites him to follow him with the following instructions: if Elisha sees him when he is caught up to be with the Lord God, the mantel will be transferred to Elisha, including the double anointing (2 Kings 2:8–10). Imagine how inspired Elisha was to be in the proximity of Elijah for years, learning and developing as a prophet of the Lord. Consider the things that he learned from Elijah in preparation for his very own earthly ministry. As a Lion leader, you influence and inspire people every day.

The question a Lion leader must answer is who have I influenced or inspired that will carry on the vision when I am gone to be with the Lord Jesus? The answer to this question can be answered by merely looking around you to see who is at your right hand. The lion knows that the reproduction of male and female lions is critical to the continued wellbeing of the pride. The male lion will carry on the DNA to the next generation, therefore, keeping the pride alive, and the female lion will be taught how to hunt, which assists with the survival of the pride.

Lion leaders, look around you. Who have you influenced?
I have influenced ________________ to be ________________.
I have influenced ________________ to do ________________.
I have influenced ________________ to go ________________.
I have influenced ________________ to achieve ________________.

The list could go on as you influence those around you. The more people you influence, the greater the probability your legacy will survive long after you retire.

SECTION 2

The Plan

This section is a deeper dive into the details of leadership and how the plan actually comes together. We will examine the perfect plan of God and the steps to developing your plan, which begins with a thought and a spoken word.

The perfect plan

Jesus, born of a virgin and given as a Son by the Father to redeem man back to the Father, God Almighty. Jesus was born with a purpose and a plan from the very beginning. This plan was established in Genesis 3:15, when God said to the serpent that He would put enmity, aggressive intentions, between it and the offspring of Eve, which will bruise the serpent's head even though the offspring, Jesus, would suffer a bruised heel. It may not sound like a plan, but there is much detail in the plan that is revealed throughout scripture.

As scripture clearly demonstrates, God Almighty had a plan to redeem man after the fall. He did not hesitate to establish this and execute on this plan. Even though we see it stretched over time, it is definitely a plan with a vision. A vision looks to the future or the end product. With the vision comes the process and steps required to make the vision possible. Notice in Luke 5:10, Jesus begins the process of calling the disciples by engaging James, John, and Peter, with the instruction to first not be fearful. Jesus would teach them to be fishers of men by utilizing their profession. These men were fishermen by occupation, who spent many hours catching fish for a living. Therefore, they knew something about fishing. Jesus doesn't lead them away from their professional knowledge but instead uses their professional knowledge as an instrument in the process of making them disciples.

Therefore, the Lion leader must take the time to understand by examination who God the Father has sent into their midst for the purpose of advancing the ministry. Taking the time to understand which gifts of each person will help with the execution of the vision. Those gifts or strengths are given to assist with the strategy. Remember how the lion forms a strategy formation in preparation to attack the gazelle? You, as the Lion leader, must consider a strategic approach to leading people.

Let's look at the strategy God used to bring down the walls of Jericho. As unorthodox as this strategy may seem from the outside looking in, it is nothing less than amazing how God almighty used Joshua in chapter 6 of the book of Joshua.

1.   March around the city of Jericho with all the armed men for six days.
2.   Have seven priest carry trumpets of ram's horns in front of the Ark.
3.   On the seventh day, march around the city of Jericho seven times with the priest blowing the trumpets.
4.   When you hear the priest blowing the long blast on the trumpets, have all the people give a loud shout.
5.   Then the walls will collapse, and the people will go up, every man straight in Jericho.

When a godly strategy is utilized, you will see the hand of God move on your behalf because it is God's plan. Notice how God's instructions were to use the priest, armed men, trumpets, and the Ark of the Covenant according to the value and skill of each. There is one more element to the strategy that we should not forget. Joshua met the angel who was the captain of the army of the Lord. The point is that Jehovah's plan includes His divine intervention, whether by Him directly or by His messengers.

1. The captain of the army of the Lord.
2. The priest carried the Ark, which represented the presence and authority of Jehovah God.
3. Seven priests, servants of Jehovah, carried and blew the trumpets in front of the Ark.
4. The people of Jehovah marched around the city with the armed guards ahead of the Ark of the Lord.
5. The rear guard, the army of Jehovah, followed the Ark of the Covenant.
6. This went on for six days as instructed by Jehovah.
7. On the seventh day, they marched seven times, which is the number of completion in the scriptures, around Jericho, and when the priest sounded the trumpet blast, Joshua commanded the people to shout.

Notice the additional details of the strategy and what a victory for the Lord God. When we carry out the plan of God exactly how He delivered the instructions with the people resources, He has given us as part of His vision and plan.

It is too often that we want to take the people the Lord God has sent to be a part of the ministry and mold them into our idea of servants. This lack of Lion leadership knowledge on how to incorporate people into the vision, plan, and strategy causes us to be selfish in our approach to leadership. This may cause people to leave our ministry and organization and move to other ministries or organizations because we are not properly utilizing their skills. It is when we recognize the strengths of an individual and how their strengths can fill the holes in our ministry, that we gain the value of the valuable people resources that our Lord God has provided us.

In John 17:8, Jesus, in His prayer to the Father, states that He gave the disciples the words He was given by the Father and the disciples accepted them. Jesus further stated that the disciples knew with certainty that He came from the Father God, and they believed that the Father God sent Him. You see, Jesus focused on the Word and knew that the Word was and is the catalyst for those who would receive it in their heart and believe it.

Now you may ask about Judas and why he did not receive and believe. Judas, as scripture points out, had his focus on the treasury. When your mind is distracted, you can't fully hear and obey the Word of God, even when He is walking with you. How do you serve both God and money? You will love one and hate the other, declares Matthew 6:24. It is shameful for us to spend so much time with the Lord in Bible study and church services and not really get to know who He is as a savior because we are so distracted. Judas was so enamored with money that he could not see the Emmanuel that walked with him every day, or maybe he did and still decided to betray Emmanuel.

We also should notice that Jesus, who is God and the Son of the Father God, who knows all things, did not push Judas out of the twelve even though Judas was not in the inner circle with Peter, James, and John. In John 12:4–6, it is stated that Judas was a thief. However, Judas was part of God's plan and the scripture fulfillment to redeem man back to God the Father as His child, through the death, burial, and resurrection of Jesus. To be a leader to a Judas takes spiritual discernment. I don't recommend everyone try to lead a Judas like Jesus did, but you must learn to hear the voice of Jesus as a sheep does its shepherd. However, I must point out Judas's value as a treasurer; he knew what to do with money.

Question

1. Do you have someone that is difficult to handle or deal with in your ministry?

   ____

   ____

2. If so, are you able to build a relationship with them?

   ____

   ____

3. How are you managing that relationship?

____

____

4. What is your plan for disciplining them?

____

____

5. What does the spirit of the Lord say about them remaining under your leadership?

____

____

6. Why is this difficult person with these skills still in your midst? What plan does God have for him/her or you?

____

____

Within a plan are several steps, and in this chapter, we will discuss how a vision and plan start with thought. These thoughts come together to make a plan that can be shared with those people resources required to be successful. We will then dig deeper into writing the vision and making it plain. This is important to the success of the ministry, team, or organization that you lead. Finally, we will discuss the need to communicate effectively and learn to delegate without feeling as though you have lost control.

Step 1: Start with a thought

Let's discuss the process of moving from a vision to a plan. A plan is the result of various ideas organized to accomplish the goals established by a vision. A plan is developed through the sharing of many thoughts and ideas.

Jeremiah 29:11–13 declares that God knows the thoughts that He thinks toward you. It seems so amazing that God Almighty thinks about you before He speaks to you, but it is true. He thinks first and, based upon His thoughts, He speaks into your life, and what God, our Father, speaks becomes the purpose, vision, and plan for you. In other words, the purpose is what you are sent to accomplish while here on earth, the vision is that which is to come to pass in the future, and the plan is the sequence of actions required to fulfill the vision.

The thought that God has for you is to "give you an expected end," as recorded in Jeremiah 29:11–13. In other words, God knows the end He has planned for you. It is no surprise to Him what your end will be because He ordained it. The point is, as a leader of God's people, God gives you a plan with a vision that He has already ordained. It is in this plan and vision that He gives you the process on how to interact with Him. He first says to call Him and He will listen to you, and those that seek Him with all their heart will find Him. Please understand the plan and vision include the comfort that comes with this relationship with the Lord. He does not forsake you but will guide you through to the vision's end.

As a leader, it is imperative that you guard your thoughts and then write them down. Your thoughts are a means by which God speaks to you and then begins to develop a plan for you and your ministry. Don't let your thoughts become fleeting thoughts that vanish into thin air. Remember, Satan wants to steal your thoughts as well as the Word of God from your mind and heart, as identified by the parable of the seed falling into the various conditions in Matthew 13:18–22.

Step 2: Write the vision

As mentioned earlier, it is important to write down your plan and vision. When you write it down, you give others the opportunity to buy into the plan and vision. This is important because others may very well want to utilize their skills to support the endeavor but are unaware of the plan and vision. Please understand that every visionary needs someone that can build and execute the vision. In the book *Start with Why* by Simon Sinek, he mentions that Bill Gates, the founder of Microsoft, needed his friend Paul Allen in more ways than one. Paul was the executer of the vision, and he could find the necessary, skilled people resources that could help with executing the dream. The point is that they were both vital to the success of the company that changed the way we utilize computers today.

When your vision is made known, it will attract the right people to assist with carrying out the plan. At Vaughn's Chapel, that is exactly what we saw when it was time to build a new church. God sent someone who was seeking a church home and had a vision. Because we were vision-focused, he was able to utilize his skills and resources to assist with bringing the vision to its expected end. If the vision had never been spoken into words and written down, no one would know about it. Get to writing, Lion leaders, and make it plain, so someone can read it and take on your passion, according to Habakkuk 2:1–3.

To further elaborate on how God works and how we, as leaders, should focus our attention on the plan and the vision, God declares the end and the result from the beginning, as shown in Isaiah 46:10. In other words, God does what we would call in the technology industry, reverse engineering, when it comes to the plan and the vision. What this means is he takes the expected final product and walks backward through time to develop the beginning and all the steps required to accomplish the desired ending, Isaiah 46:10. Now, I know Jehovah does not have to walk backward through time to develop the plan, but that is the best way I can think of to help you understand the power of God's plan.

As a Lion leader, you must take time to think about the expected results and then think backward, as led by the holy spirit of God, who searches the deep things of God and reveals them to you (1 Corinthians 2:10). The Holy Spirit will show you things to come out of the deep treasury of our Lord. When the Holy Spirit reveals the things of God, you should be ready to write them down and implement the processes. Don't get worried about the needed resources because Isaiah 46:8–11 declares that God can call a man from a foreign country to bring to pass His purposes. This is exciting when we understand that God works according to a plan and a vision that have been engineered in reverse to meet the requirements He has set in motion.

Step 3: Communicate

As a Lion leader, when your thoughts become words, you are engaged in communication. Communication is vital to leading people. Communication has two parts: one speaks while the other listens and vice versa. Communication is a two-way street that both parties must participate in equally. When communication breaks down, we get lectures, and most people don't like being lectured. As a leader, it is important to allow others to think and express their thoughts equally. The final decision is yours as the leader because you are ultimately responsible. However, godly council from those that make up your team or leadership organization is in order and an expected practice.

When a lion roars, what is he saying? He is communicating that he is awake and ready to hunt and defend his territory. The lion roar can be heard three to five miles away by every mammal, including man, according to *National Geographic*. The lion is further communicating to other lions that this is his domain, so beware. As he keeps watch over his territory, this ferocious creature demands respect, and trespassers, beware.

By the way, did you know that prayer is how you communicate with God and how he communicates with you? Prayer is you giving God the Father the earthly permission to intervene in your life here on earth, in the Name and character of Jesus? Yes, I said give God, the Almighty Creator, permission. Yes, I know God can wipe man out with the sound of His voice, which is like many waters, but God Jehovah wants you to have such a relationship with Him that you invite Him into your house. God Jehovah throughout history has used man to execute His will here on earth and has required us to pray and seek His face while turning from our wicked ways (2 Chronicles 7:15). He merely needs a willing vessel like you, His ordained minister and servant.

The Plan

1. What thoughts or ideas do you have that can be developed into a vision or a plan?

   ____

   ____

2. What thoughts or ideas do you have from the Holy Spirit that you have not executed yet?

   ____

   ____

3. Who around you has planted a thought or idea into your mind, and how can they assist with the beginning stages of its development?

   ____

   ____

4. To whom have you shared the plan that makes up the vision?

   ____

   ____

Step 4: Delegate authority

To delegate means to send someone in your place. If you never learn to delegate, you will do everything yourself. Many leaders are impeded because they will not relinquish authority and power to others that are willing vessels. We pray for our Lord to send servants, but when they show up, we put them out to pasture because we don't know how to properly utilize them. We become afraid that they are going to take over, or worse yet, misrepresent the vision and the plan. A Lion leader that knows how to lead is not afraid but operates in the power of God of the Holy Spirit without fear, states 2 Timothy 1:7. When a Lion leader, or any Christian for that matter, is afraid, they are operating in doubt and unbelief. When this occurs, the Lion leader will not finish what God has ordained him to do.

In Matthew 28:18–20, Jesus transfers authority to the disciples because, after the crucifixion, He is going to sit at the right hand of the Father. The disciples have the responsibility of taking the gospel to the world. They further have the responsibility of teaching and baptizing in the name of the Father, the Son, and the Holy Ghost, all those that would believe, making them disciples also. This sounds like a tall task, but Jesus finishes the discourse by saying, "I will be with you always, even to the end of the ages." In other words, as a leader, though you have delegated responsibility, you can keep your eye on the effort without taking the reins from those that are willing and able to assist with the plan and vision. Lion leaders must realize that Jesus will send those that will be a part of the solution and not part of the problem or cause a problem. That is not to say problematic members will not join the team because they are skilled as well and believe they can add value. If and when that occurs, as a leader, you will need to know how to handle them as well.

Jesus demonstrates the principle of delegation in Luke 9:1–6, when he calls the twelve together and gives them both power and authority. Power is the ability to execute a miracle, and authority is the permission required to execute the miracle. The disciples operated in both power and authority when they went forth into the cities and performed many miracles. Lion leaders must learn and exercise this basic principle if they are going to grow beyond the status quo. Jesus further teaches that not everyone will receive you or what you have to offer, but don't worry, shake the dust off your feet, and keep it moving.

There was another occasion in Matthew 17:19–20 where the disciples came to Jesus to gain an understanding as to why they could not cast out the demon from the boy. Jesus takes the opportunity to teach them about the aspects of faith and how, with faith the size of a mustard seed, they could say to the mountain, be removed from its current place to another place and it shall be done. Be ready for those teaching moments when you can pour into those that God has sent for you to lead. The lion leader is always teaching the cubs how to hunt when they are young because they have the responsibility to carry on the bloodline. There are times when the male lion will play with the cubs, but even in their play time, they are learning valuable lessons that will help to save their lives.

1. To whom can you delegate authority?

   ____

   ____

2. What is hindering your ability to delegate authority?

   ____

   ____

3. Who will carry on the work you have started?

   ____

   ____

Conclusion

Write down the thoughts that God the Father has for you. Make them plain so that those people resource He will send to assist you with the vision will have something to run with. With this vision in mind, you will be able to properly communicate what needs to be done and where to properly utilize those needed skills.

It is important that you are walking by faith and staying positive because others can read in your eyes fear, uncertainty, and doubt. No one wants to join in a vision that is already defeated from the beginning, and no one wants to follow a leader that is unsure.

Finally, transfer both power and authority to those that are willing to join your team. Trust them to complete the task while you observe them without taking the reins away from them. Be ready to provide constructive criticism while utilizing their skills to move the effort along.

SECTION 3

Developing Your Lion Mentality/ Leadership Skills

Leadership skills are something that every leader assumes they have until they are put into a real-world situation where they have to utilize those untrained skills. My first few months as a pastor were an indication that I had a bit to learn about being a pastor, not to mention a leader. The Lord sent me to a seasoned church with deacons, trustees, and mothers that were accustomed to leading by seniority, which was not the way I was exposed to church leadership. They were a very strong-willed group of men and women, all with different personalities and different ideas of leadership. I had to learn who was the leader of the leaders, and that included family members. Which family had the greatest influence and which family went along with which family? Then there was the gossip that was born from the various factions of the church family. It was an interesting first five years as pastor and leader of this church that did not have a vision and did not have money in the bank to implement anything, even if there was a vision.

In this chapter, I want to discuss a four-step action plan that will help you with developing the Lion leadership mentality that will aid you in leading and developing Lion leaders. Please note that each church family is different, and each leader is different; however, there are some principles that are universal and apply across church denominations.

Step 1: Accept godly counsel

What I had to learn first and foremost was to accept godly advice from a godly man whom I trusted to pour into my life. He assisted me with developing into a pastor and a Lion leader who could lead the church family deeper into the kingdom of God by executing godly principles. Therefore, I learned to accept advice from a pastor and leader who would adopt me as his son in the ministry. Dr. Logan Carson was that Lion leader. He had led several churches in advancing the kingdom of God. He was a professor at Southeastern Theological Seminary in Wake Forest, North Carolina, and had been pastoring longer than I had been alive. He was a wise Lion leader and pastor, and I was so glad to be able to sit down with him and share a plate of croaker while discussing the things that had made him a successful church leader. He had my best interests in mind without a hidden agenda. He taught me how to present a plan that would be acceptable to the congregation and how to move past the biases in order to move the plan and vision of God forward. He taught me how to be positive in the midst of adversity and how to have faith when doubters were around you due to fear. He was such a positive influence who I miss dearly today. No one has come along to take his place as my earthly mentor. Therefore, I take the opportunity to pour into others that require godly counsel.

When we would meet at his home, he would say how are the Vaughn's Chapelites, which was my open door to share what was going on. I learned so much from being around him; just being in his presence was special and enlightening. Every leader needs a mentor and advisor who will hold you accountable, someone you can bounce ideas off or just share a good meal with. I encourage you to carefully select a godly man or woman who can be a part of your inner circle.

In 1 Samuel 3:1–10, Eli teaches Samuel that the voice that is calling him is the Lord God Almighty. Samuel is not accustomed to hearing the voice of God; therefore, he needs a godly leader to instruct him how to answer the voice of the Lord. I have found some leaders and pastors find it hard to accept godly counsel, and perhaps for good reason. They become jaded by those that seek to do them more harm than good, even in the church that they lead. There are others that offer advice but have hidden agendas that can go against what you believe is the will of God. That's where spiritual discernment comes in and you learn to eat the chicken and leave the bone, as they say here in North Carolina. In other words, learn to analyze a conversation and determine what is good for you and what does not work for you. It is this skill of discernment that will be a sieve, and with the Holy Spirit as a guide, you will be able to determine what benefits you and the ministry you serve.

There were times in my thirty years of pastorate where someone wanted to advise me on something based upon their experience. It usually started out with the phrase, "You need to," or "This is what we should do." These phrases always made me cringe because I knew what was coming next. Advice on how I should carry out a task without any intention of helping with the recommendation that was just given. I would respectfully listen and end the conversation with a suggestion of my own by asking them to develop the plan and get back to me. I believe, as a leader, that if you have a suggestion, you should be able to implement it.

Case Study: Moses

Let's look at Moses, his father-in-law, Jethro, and how Jethro suggested an approach to leading the children of Israel that numbered over five hundred thousand men. No matter how you count it, that was a lot of people to govern, lead, and advise, but God put them all under Moses's authority. Thank God for godly advice from a priest. In Exodus 18:17–22, Jethro asks Moses to listen and comprehend what he is about to say on the matter of leading such a large number of people. But not only that, but also Jethro tells Moses that God shall be with him as he follows this approach.

The first thing Moses had to do was to teach them the ordinances and laws. The leaders were not appointed until they were taught and learned the ordinances and laws of God Almighty. This is important because potential leaders need to understand what they can and cannot do in the church, according to the Bible, church policy, and church bylaws. These are boundaries that we all have to work within because, without boundaries, there is chaos. That is not to say you can't change boundaries as your community changes or your membership changes, but you must have boundaries to govern how you will operate. The Bible is just that: the boundaries that Jehovah has determined we should live within in order to please him. We, as humans, have a choice to live within the boundaries of His word or live outside His word and accept the consequences.

Church bylaws are like ground rules; they are the policies that you and the church or organization will operate under. These rules are there to establish the boundaries that reflect your values. Remember, values are those things that you hold dear to your heart and those things that you will not break or deviate from. I am not suggesting that you implement so many rules that you can't keep up with them, but determine the limits that you are willing to go to, and if you need to modify those limits based upon some unforeseen circumstances, then you can do that.

For example, we as a church have bylaws, which were given so we can govern how we operate as a church, one of which is a mandatory monthly business meeting. When COVID-19 hit us in March 2020, we were not meeting as a church; therefore, we did not have monthly business meetings. The decision was made to meet with only the deacons, trustees, assistant pastor, and pastor. Those meetings were handled via video conference as well. I fully expected the membership to be okay with that, at least for a while. The point is that the decision was made because of an unforeseen, extenuating circumstance. As a Lion leader, you can make those decisions that are in the best interest of the organization and with godly counsel from those around you.

Now back to Moses. Moses then had to teach the Israelites how to walk worthy. The walk is more of how to live every day, before the people that you have rule over. The steps of a good man are ordered by the Lord, according to Psalm 37:23. It is important that we choose leaders that know the word of God and know Him well enough to walk worthily in His presence and yours as their leader. Now that is not to say leaders don't make mistakes, because leaders do make mistakes. The difference is, can you ask for forgiveness and get back to the purpose that Jehovah has called you to?

Next, Moses is to select men who fear and reverence God Almighty. Men who know the truth and operate in the truth. Men who are not covetous of other people and their possessions. These men had a great responsibility; therefore, it was imperative that they grow in the Lord by studying the word of God.

Finally, Moses begins describing the work that must be done. Moses is now able to separate his work of the ministry to handle the hard issues and bring them to the Lord God, versus the work of the ministry that the chosen leaders will handle daily. This process took a load off Moses and allowed the load to be distributed across many leaders instead of just him. Delegation is critical to leadership because we leaders tend to want to do everything ourselves, or worse, we have the tendency to think that no one can do it better. That is why I believe many pastors and leaders don't last long before they seek a new pulpit from which to preach.

The Lion mentality seeks godly counsel because the Lion leader already knows that doing everything on their own is not viable. The Lion leader is particular about who is allowed to advise, and the Lion leader is able to discern what is good advice for the organization or ministry. As you continue to develop the Lion mentality, you will surround yourself with those that can pour into your life just like you pour into others' lives. Jesus poured so much into Peter, James, and John that after He resurrected, they carried the gospel message with the same vigor that He did during the three years of His ministry. Please understand, when you, as a Lion leader, make disciples, your ministry and legacy live on in them.

Legacy is one thing that may be a second thought by leaders because their focus is on short-term gains and not on the purpose, vision, and plan from Jehovah. The legacy of a Lion leader is lived on and carried on by those that are disciples, trained, mentored, and developed into the future Lion leaders. Who are you training?

Step 2: Select the leadership team

Developing teams is very important, and how you develop that team is even more important. Let's look at the teams that most churches have. There is the: ministerial team, deacon or steward team, usher team, music team, hospitality team, security team, kitchen team, armor bearer team, children's church team, and perhaps many more. How do you assimilate all these teams to work for the common goal of the vision and plan of the church? The answer is understanding the value each team member and team brings to the vision and plan, and how each individual leader can assist with accomplishing those objectives.

Your role as a Lion leader is to lead the leaders and not everyone within those teams. If you try to be the leader for each team, department, or auxiliary, you will burn out because everyone will come to you for everything. That practice undermines the authority of the leader of the team, organization, or auxiliary. Yes, there are times when you must step in to get things moving, but resist the urge to take over. Remember, each leader has a strength, therefore, depend upon those individual strengths to accomplish the goals. As a leader, your responsibility is to coach the leaders that coach the individuals on the team.

As a leader, you must seek the Lord for the team that He has appointed you to implement the vision and plan. Even if that means the Lord must send people from other places to serve on your team. When God the Father answers your prayer for people resources, ask Him to reveal to you why He has sent a certain person or people. On several occasions, we wanted to improve the choir's performance and push them to the next level. The Lord sent a music teacher and professional from Virginia to assist us, and did she push the choir? Oh yes! Those that thought they could sing began to see that they had a range that was untapped. On another occasion, the Lord moved a local musician and teacher to be the instrument in His hands. This musician pushed the choir members once more, and during these sessions, one of the members told him, "No, I can't hit that octave." He was not having it and pushed anyway, and boy, did she go up an octave and did it very well. I love how our Lord moves over the face of the earth with power and authority, affecting our lives in the process of His mighty move.

The point is, God knows the plans he has for you and the appointed member of your team has not arrived yet, but God can call a person from the far east to assist with His plan (Isaiah 46:10–11). When a Lion leader gets this revelation in his heart and learns to trust the Lord God and Father of all, he will begin to grow in leaps and bounds. The Lion leader will then see God do exceedingly and abundantly above all that you ask or think, according to the power working within him (Ephesians 3:20–21).

Now that you have your team selected, you must put in the time to train them, just as Jesus did with the disciples. Jesus did the training of the disciples as on-the-job training, meaning He demonstrated the task of healing and casting out demons and then told them to perform the same task. Mark 6:7 records the event of Jesus sending out the disciples two by two with authority and power to cast out spirits—perhaps one of the most difficult tasks known to man and the simplest tasks known to Jesus the Christ. Jesus taught them that His authority and power was over both the spiritual and physical. Therefore, He wanted the disciples to know and understand this simple principle.

The Lion mentality seeks to develop the leaders around him based upon the strengths of the individual. These strengths allow the individual to perform at their highest level because this is typically their passion area. The Lion mentality also seeks to develop teams that can join in the purpose, vision, and plan because they have a deep-rooted similar passion. Remember that a pride of lions works strategically to accomplish their goal, and they all have their role to play in the vision and plan to survive. Jesus, the Lion of Judah, was able to take twelve men with various occupations and make them disciples. The Lion mentality seeks to take men and women who perhaps would not ordinarily be selected and make them Lion leaders, teaching them so they can teach others. Therefore, making disciples or other Lion leaders.

Step 3: Making Lion leaders

As a Lion leader, you will encounter many different types of people and leaders that desire to join God's vision and plan that have been given to you. Jesus had Peter, the rambunctious and boisterous disciple, who was the first to jump in line and speak up while using his sword to cut off a person's ear (John 18:10). Jesus also had James, the brother of John, who represents the family in the church. Sometimes, to many leaders, family members can be scary because they can form an alliance against you, reminding you that they knew you when or before you were a leader or pastor. Jesus did not worry about such an ordeal; He gave them all the same word. Jesus also had John the beloved. John would stay close to Jesus and rest his head on Jesus's chest, demonstrating his love for Jesus the Christ (John 13:23). John wanted to be so close to Jesus that he would hear His heartbeat.

Then there is Judas, the son of perdition, who would betray Jesus, and Jesus knew it (John 17:12). Jesus did not send Judas, the avaricious disciple, away because scripture needed to be fulfilled. What do I mean, you ask? Acts 1:16 declares that David spoke of Judas and how he would betray the Messiah. When God gives a prophetic word, it must come to pass, even when human logic can make no sense of it. When God gives you a vision, wait on it until it comes to pass. This is what I mean; a vision has its present tense, which means it is spoken in the current season but executable in the future season. Just because a vision is delayed does not mean it is forgotten. Consider Ezekiel 12:25; God declares that He will no longer delay, and He will speak His word and perform it. Be very sure that when God our Father speaks, He will perform just what He said.

The vision becomes visible over time, and the plan is executed step-by-step. Disciplining Lions is a process of teaching them what you have been taught and then empowering them to develop as you have developed as a leader. Lion leaders make Lion leaders just like disciples make disciples. Have you noticed that Jesus pulled Peter, James, and John into His inner circle? These three were with him at the mount of transfiguration, where the Father God, Elijah, and Moses were present. It was Peter that Jesus asked, "Who do you say that I am?" in Matthew 16:13–19. Peter declared that "You are the Christ," and he answered correctly as directed by the Heavens, the inner voice of God the Father. This inner circle truly was a benefit to the three disciples because they had the greatest teacher, Jesus, who is one with the Father God. Everybody needs somebody at some point in time, so why not put some time into seeking the right person through prayer.

Step 4: Communication

Communication is such a vital aspect of leadership that we sometimes take it for granted. If you don't communicate and communicate well, the team will not know what is on your mind, no matter how anointed they are. When you communicate, you are giving the team permission to participate in the plan and vision. Therefore, you are giving them the power to utilize their skills to carry out the plan and vision.

As a visionary Lion leader, you don't have the skills or knowledge to do everything; you need those that can get things done based upon the vision and plan. Communication does not stop with one meeting; it continues throughout the process of the execution of the vision and plan. The more you communicate, the clearer the vision and plan become, and the smoother the process will be because this gives you the opportunity to create a rapport with the lions in one-on-one or group sessions. For example, there may be occasions where one-on-one sessions are required by the leader of a team because this allows for a more personal touch.

Remember, communication occurs when one person is talking and the other is listening, followed by the latter person talking while the former listens. The intent of communication is to share ideas or to reveal issues that need to be addressed. As a Lion leader, it is best to be a better listener than a problem solver. I find that most people know the answer to the problem; they just need someone with whom to talk it through by asking the right questions. You become the sounding board that asks questions to stimulate critical thinking and problem-solving.

The Lion mentality learns to listen and listen well. Today we are quick to solve the problem, leaving the person dependent upon you to solve the next problem and the next problem. It is an irresistible urge to solve a person's problem, even when you don't have all the details, because it stimulates your sense of accomplishment, making you feel good inside. And who does not want to feel good inside? However, with the Lion Mentality, the leader does not solve the problems for the team but rather acts as a facilitator, asking questions that stimulate the knowledge-seeker's brain, challenging them to answer their own questions and dive deeper into their own minds and experiences, answering the questions and solving their problems based upon their personal vantage point. The Lion leader not only communicates verbally but is also able to read body language, therefore, interpreting signals that are unspoken, which are vital to the successful communication of the vision and the plan.

Step 5: Group development

Now that you have formed the team, shared the vision, and taught them how to execute the plan, it is time to understand the basic stages of team development. Each team, according to Daniel Levy in his book *Group Dynamics for Teams*, when teams are first formed, they go through the following stages: forming, storming, norming, performing, and adjourning. I will explain each one accordingly.

Stage 1
Forming

When a team first comes together, they don't know each other, so they exchange pleasantries while feeling out each other. This is the time for you to introduce yourself, the vision, and plan while creating an environment that is conducive to the communication of ideas. If you don't create the correct environment, the extroverts will dominate the meeting while the introverts will sit back and listen and disengage. That will become a recipe for disaster because the introverts have great ideas as well, but you must encourage and assure them that their voices are welcome and expected. In a leadership training session, I was identified as an introvert, and as a result, I had to learn to push through my hindrances and speak up when I had an idea or opinion that could benefit the group. This is something a lion leader must recognize in a group and encourage the introverts to participate in the exercises and create opportunities for everyone to participate equally.

Stage 2
Storming

The next stage is *Storming*, which occurs when members start to communicate their feelings but are not yet working together to deliver the required results of the vision and plan. When everyone is acting independently, it can become problematic and diminish the power of the group. As the Lion leader, you must work to get beyond this stage because unchecked personalities could cause the team to be less productive. Since you understand this is a stage, don't give up; work your way through it by staying focused on the vision and the plan. Refocus the group if they get off track, and lead by example. They will appreciate your passion and commitment to the cause, and if they are true followers of your passion, you will get to the next stage, *norming*. This is the point where the Lion leader is the glue for everyone involved. The Lion must assess the participants and help to guide the personalities to begin to come together as a collective group. This can be done by drawing everyone's focus to why you are assembled and how every member of the team is a valuable contributing factor in the vision, plan, and process.

Stage 3
Norming

It is in the *Norming* stage that people find their role and how they can contribute to the overall vision. It is here that you, as the Lion leader, will be able to see the strengths of the individuals and how each person's strengths contribute to the vision and plan. It is even more important that you let the team know their areas of responsibility and for what you will be holding them accountable, which easily eliminates the guesswork for the team members. Also, remember to give positive reinforcement along the way. Recognition is vital to the success of the team and will go a long way toward creating longevity among the team members.

Stage 4
Performing

The *Performing* stage is where the work gets done because the team has gelled, and everyone is on the same page with the ability to see the end goal. There is less behavior that is intended to impress because you dealt with that in the storming stage. This stage is where you, as a leader, watch the participants go to work and perform as you knew they could.

Stage 5
Adjourning

The final stage is *Adjourning*, which is critical because you want to take time to recognize the efforts and contributions of the team. We sometimes take for granted that these may be volunteer hours and time away from family. Appreciate them for what they have done, love on them a bit, and you will have participants for the next major project. As a matter of fact, they will ask you what is next.

When the Lion leader has a plan to make Lion leaders and empower them to produce by using strong communication skills that allow for the proper understanding of the task, the Lion leader will see a productive team. When these Lion leaders that you are developing come together for the common goal of carrying out the vision and plan, the Lion leader will do like Jesus and get more done in a shorter period of time. When all is said and done, the Lion leader must be focused on making other Lions just like him, therefore, developing someone that will take the vision to the next steps in the process, just as Joshua did after the death of Moses.

SECTION 4

Catching and Leading Lions with the Jesus Method

Jesus took twelve men of various occupations and asked them to become his disciples. These disciples would give up their occupations to follow a man they had just met with a plan from God, whom they would call Father.

Going Fishing

In Matthew 4:18, after Jesus has been tempted by the devil, he calls four fishermen, two of whom are Simon (who would eventually be called Peter) and Andrew, his brother, who were fishermen. It should be noted that fishing was a fruitful occupation that brought the families much gain. Jesus merely said to these fishermen in verse 19, "Follow me and I will make you fishers of men," and they immediately stopped what they were doing and followed Jesus. Why would men with a profitable occupation give it up to follow a man named Jesus? What was it about Jesus that pressed upon them to make such a decision? The answer is in the verse, "make you fishers of men."

Jesus was not asking them to do something they had never done before. He was asking them to fish for men by learning to use a different bait. Jesus came to them with a plan and a willingness to teach them what He knew about and something they did not know. The word *make* means to produce by affecting the mind or the way a person thinks about something. Jesus was going to set them on a course that would turn the world upside down.

The other two men Jesus called were James and John, the sons of Zebedee. These men were fishermen as well. Are you seeing a theme here? Jesus is choosing men that understand work, service, and teamwork. Surely, if you don't work together on a fishing ship, you could be in a world of hurt and trouble. These brothers immediately left their ship and followed Jesus.

Let's look at the details in Luke 5:1–11, where Jesus has a multitude following him and He asks Peter to launch his ship out from the shore a bit while He teaches. Peter takes this opportunity to inform Jesus that they had fished all night and caught nothing. Jesus instructs him to let down his net, and Peter begrudgingly did so. Miraculously, he caught a sum of fish so large that they had to ask for help from James and John, who were on a neighboring ship and partners with Peter and Andrew. There were so many fish that both ships nearly sank; oh, what a catch!

Peter now realizes who Jesus is and falls down at Jesus's feet and repents, asking Jesus to leave him for he was a sinful man. But did Peter fall down because he recognized Jesus as the savior, or did he recognize Jesus for the miracle He performed in causing such a catch with their nets? Luke 5:9 tells us that Peter and all were astonished by the draught of fish that was taken in. It was a miracle only the Son of God or God the Creator could perform with such power and authority.

Notice in Luke 5:27, when He calls a man named Levi, who was a publican and not a fisherman, to follow him. The publican was a collector of taxes and more than likely a wealthy one because he scraped a few extra dollars off for himself. As it would be noted in Luke, when Jesus calls him and he accepts, Levi throws a great feast at his home and invites a large number of publicans and other sinners. Notice that Jesus chose someone who could reach another portion of the population, the publicans. Who better to reach the publicans than a fellow publican? Again, the passion of Jesus was to redeem man back to the Father by using the skills of the publican. Leaders, please take note: if you want to catch a bird, you have to think like a bird, and you need a teacher that thinks like a bird to teach you how to catch birds. Simply stated, like understands like, therefore someone from a unique background could be a very strong instrument in the hands of any Lion leader. Therefore, based upon your call to ministry, God the Father may very well send you people that will serve in a capacity that specifically meets the requirements of the vision.

Conclusion

It is important to note that a person with a skill is just a person with a skill, but a person with a skill that is anointed by the Lord is an immensely different discussion. Moses had such an experience from the Lord when he was to build the tabernacle. In Exodus 35:30–35, God anointed Bezaleel, the son of Uri, by filling him with the spirit of God, in wisdom, understanding, knowledge, and in all manner of workmanship. It is important to have skilled men that have been anointed by God to carry out His will and way. We, as leaders, must be able to recognize such skilled, anointed men in the ministry because it is important to get the job done.

In their book *Now, Discover Your Strengths* by Marcus Buckingham and Donald O. Clifton PhD, the authors focus on teaching leaders how to identify the strengths of those that they lead. This approach is interesting because its focus is not on the weakness of the individual but on the strength of the person being led. They have found that when you focus on the strengths of the person, you get more production out of them, and they are happier doing what they like best. As Lion leaders, it is important that we understand this while focusing on the strengths of the servants that our Father God sends us. Lion leaders should take some time to get to know those valuable people resources and how they fit into the spiritual puzzle we call ministry. God the Father did not send them to be under your responsibility just to occupy a chair. Think about it. Take a moment to list the names of those you lead and write down their strengths. If you don't know their strength, schedule a one-on-one to get to know them.

Name	Role in Church or Organization	Strength of the Servant of the Lord
1.		
2.		
3.		
4.		
5.		
6.		
7.		

Let's review what we have learned. First, identify your purpose or passion, making sure it fits in with the vision. Secondly, relay the plan, which are the steps to fulfill the purpose and the vision. Thirdly, seek skilled men that have been anointed to carry out the vision and plan with the same passion you have. The Holy Spirit will reveal such people to you and show you how He has chosen them to be profitable to you. Finally, determine the strengths of the men and women, including how their strengths contribute to your vision, plan, and passion.

REMARKS FROM THE AUTHOR

Thank God for the Lion of Judah who won the war of sin in the flesh and gave His life so we could have life and have it more abundantly. Thank God the Father for Jesus, the resurrected Savior, who not only had values but also valued the plan of God to redeem man, that He allowed the Roman soldiers to beat Him until flesh was torn from His body with blood running down His face and body. Thank God the Father for Jesus, who carried the cross of shame, where He would be nailed to between two sinners. Thank God the Father for Jesus, who valued the plan of God the Father so much that even near death, *forgave* a sinner on the cross and proclaimed that on that day he would be with Him in paradise. Thank You, Jesus, for holding to the value of *serving* the Lord God our Father in the resurrection, for the grave-rendering death with no sting, and the grave without victory. Thank You, Jesus, for demonstrating the value of *obedience* by resurrecting as You were commanded by the Father in John 10:17–18 and now sitting on the right hand of the Father forever interceding for us the believer. Thank You, Father God, Jesus the Son of God, and the Holy Spirit, for *loving* us so much that You died, was buried, and resurrected for us!

ABOUT THE AUTHOR

Lynwood Batts was born in Wilson County, North Carolina, to parents Allan Harris and Magdalene Batts. He grew up playing with cousins and working on his grandfather's farm. His grandfather was a preacher and pastor in the Primitive Baptist Association.

In 1984, Batts heard the call of God to preach the gospel while living in Syracuse, New York. He later returned to North Carolina, where he received the call to pastor at Vaughn's Chapel Missionary Baptist Church in Elm City. It is there that he continues to develop disciples that have the *lion mentality*.